Alzheimer's

by Pat Duff
Author, Artist and Poet

Copyright © 2018 by Pat Duff

All rights reserved. No part of this publication may be used or reproduced in any manner without the permission of the author.

Published by folioDetroit.com

ISBN-13: 978-1717188632
ISBN-10: 171718863X

Contents

The Seven Warning Signs of Alzheimer's Disease 5

The Seven Stages of Alzheimer's Disease. 7

Alzheimer's 9

Are You Sleeping? 11

Dementia 13

Dementia II 15

Life in Bits and Pieces 17

Waiting to Die. 19

You Once Were Young 21

The Artwork 23

The Seven Warning Signs of Alzheimer's Disease

1. Progressive Memory Loss
    a. Impairment of short-term memory
    b. Then long-term memory
    c. Then no memory
2. Decline in Cognitive Abilities
    a. Problem solving
    b. Judgment
    c. Logic
3. Change in Mood or Personality
    a. Withdrawn, irritable, inexplicably
    b. Hostile, apathetic, confused, and anxious
    c. Depression
4. Speech Impairment
    a. Difficulty finding words
5. Behavioral problems
6. Sundowning—worsen in late afternoon & evening
    a. Stubborness
    b. Resistance of care
    c. Obscene language
7. Impairment of basic motor skills (Apraxia)
    a. Cannot dress themselves
    b. Cannot use electronic devices
    c. Later stages—difficulty sitting in a chair, chewing, or walking

The Seven Stages of Alzheimer's Disease

1. No impairment: during this stage Alzheimer's Disease is not detectable and no memory problem or other symptoms of dementia are evident.
2. Very mild decline.
3. Mild decline.
4. Moderate decline.
5. Moderately severe decline.
6. Severe decline.
7. Very severe decline.

Alzheimer's

I cried as I left him
So helpless and not
   With the world.
He doesn't know that
   I'm gone,
Just that I'll be there
   Tomorrow,
Maybe.
How long will it be before
   He forgets me forever?
I love you my Alzheimer's
   Husband.
Stay with me as long as you
   Can.

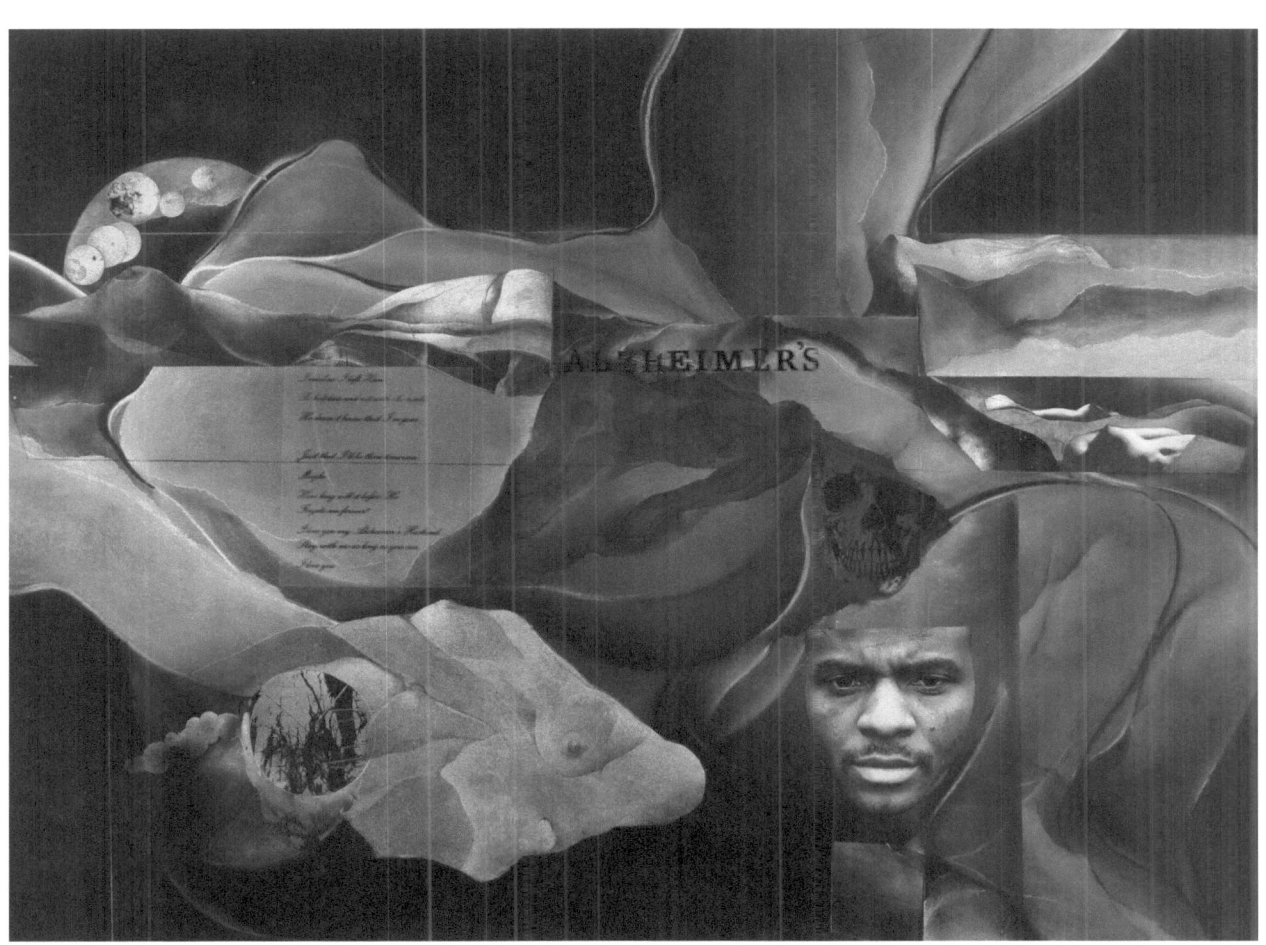

"Alzheimer's", Charcoal

Are You Sleeping?

Are you sleeping
    Or just existing?
You lay there still...
Not quite dead,
    Or are you...
In a coffin or in
    A bed?
For no one knows
    You're here,
Not you, nor them,
    For what?
Do they care?
Do they know?
Why are you
    Forgotten?

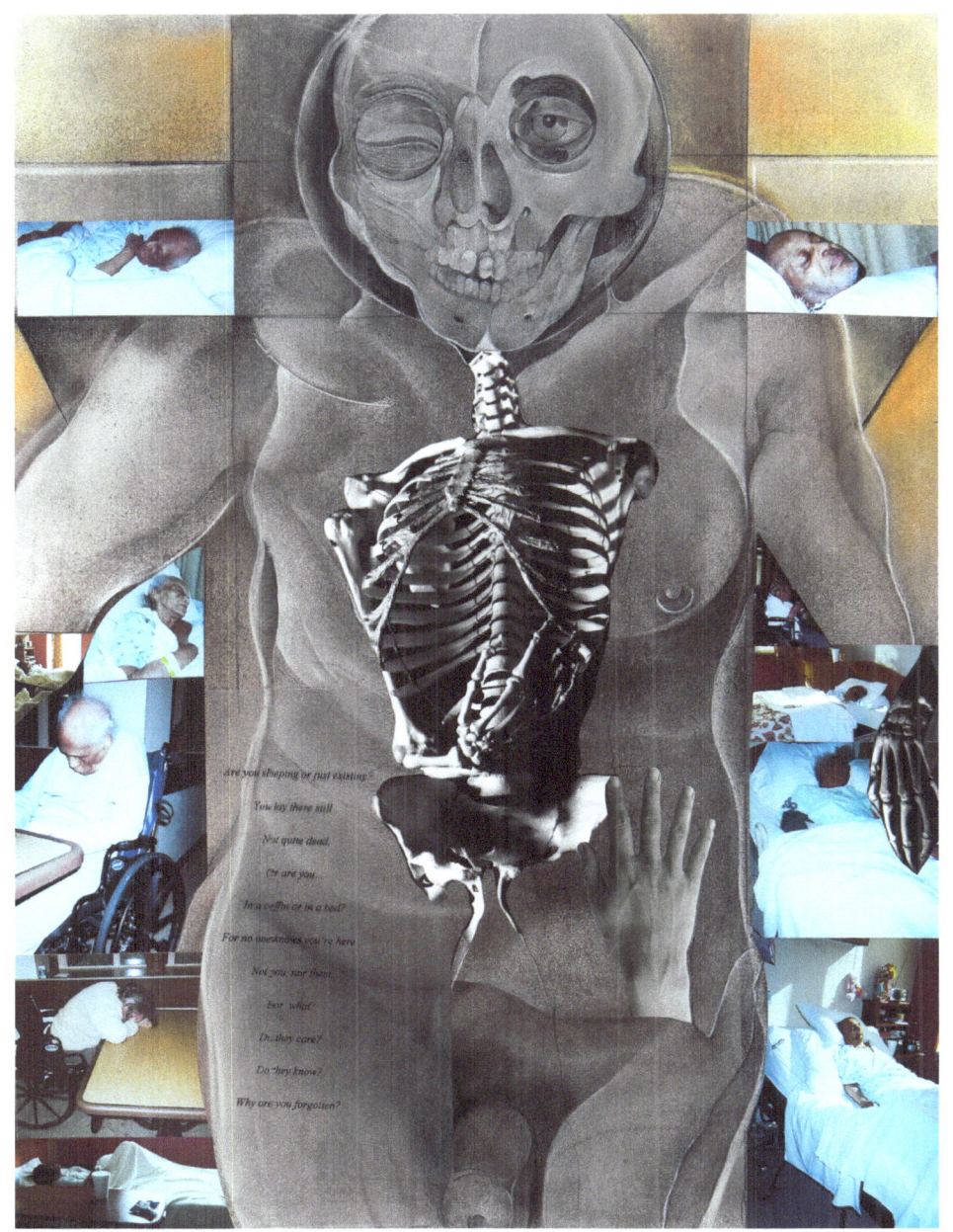

"Are You Sleeping?", Charcoal & Pastel

Dementia

You look at me
    With dark
Penetrating eyes,
Beckoning...
I try to resist
But you engulf
    My soul...
I succumb to fate,
For you have taken
    Control.
The body ages,
The mind is gone,
Life ceases.

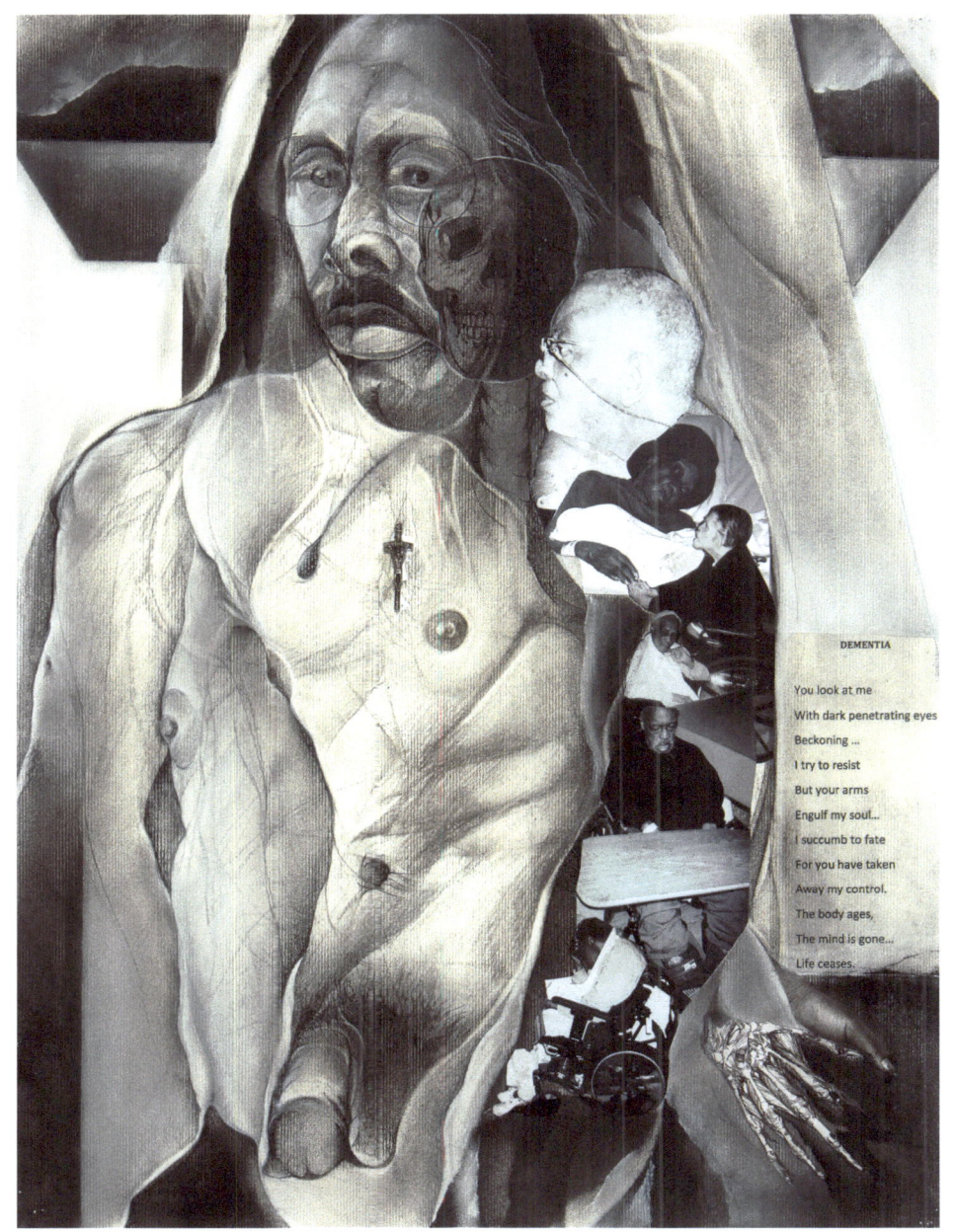

"Dementia", Charcoal

Dementia II

Here lies a shell of a man,
Someone I used to know!
There is little of him left,
But not the one I knew.
What is the purpose of
His existence now?
Or is it just my past
Remembrances of us,
Or my waiting for his
Demise?

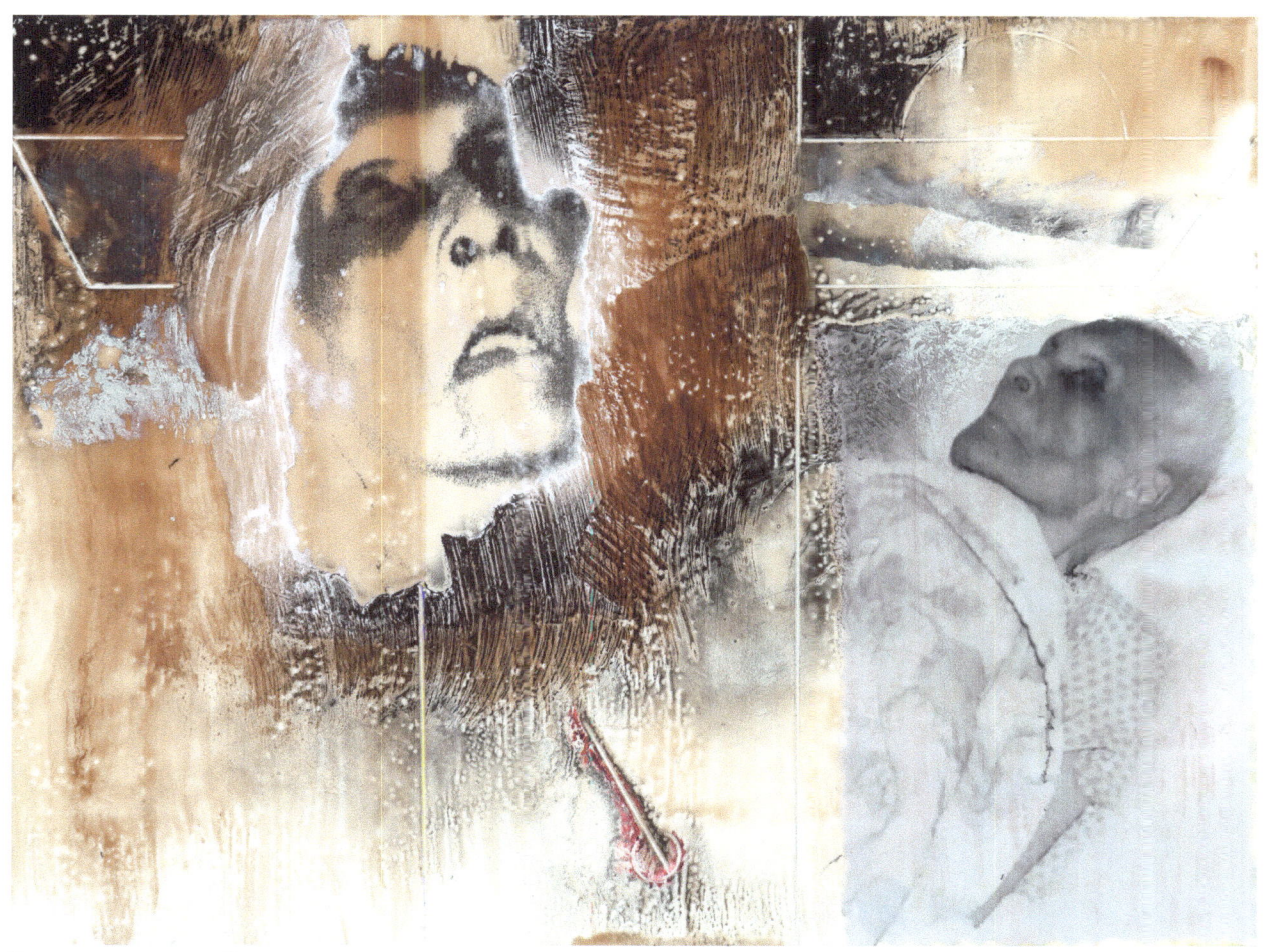

"Dementia II", Encaustic

Life in Bits and Pieces

We are born...
Live Life in Bits and Pieces,
Love someone...flowers,
Cry sometimes...thorns,
And then we...
Spiral down,
Disintegrate.

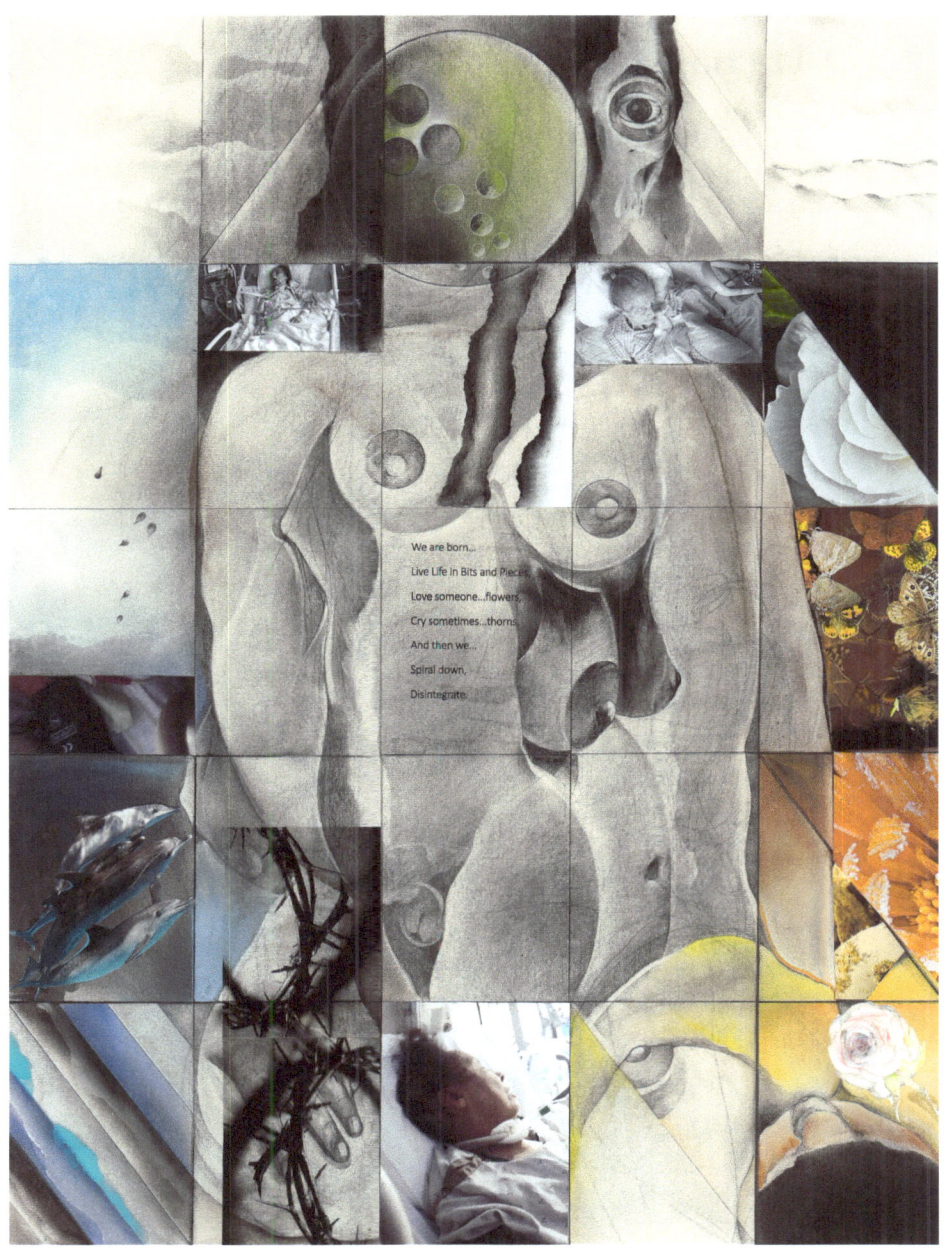

"Life in Bits and Pieces", Charcoal & Pastel

Waiting to Die

I see them every day
Huddled over in their
Wheelchairs,
Some staring
   Aimlessly,
Others asleep.
Waiting to die,
Isn't that what they
   Do?
For most there are
   No visitors,
No one stops by.
For what purpose?
Is their life already
   Spent?
Did they make their
   Fortune?
Did they love
   Someone?
Did they make a
   Difference in
   The world?
Or are they just in it
   As they are now?
Most don't remember
   Where they are,
Or who they might be.
They just exist,
And we have forgotten them.

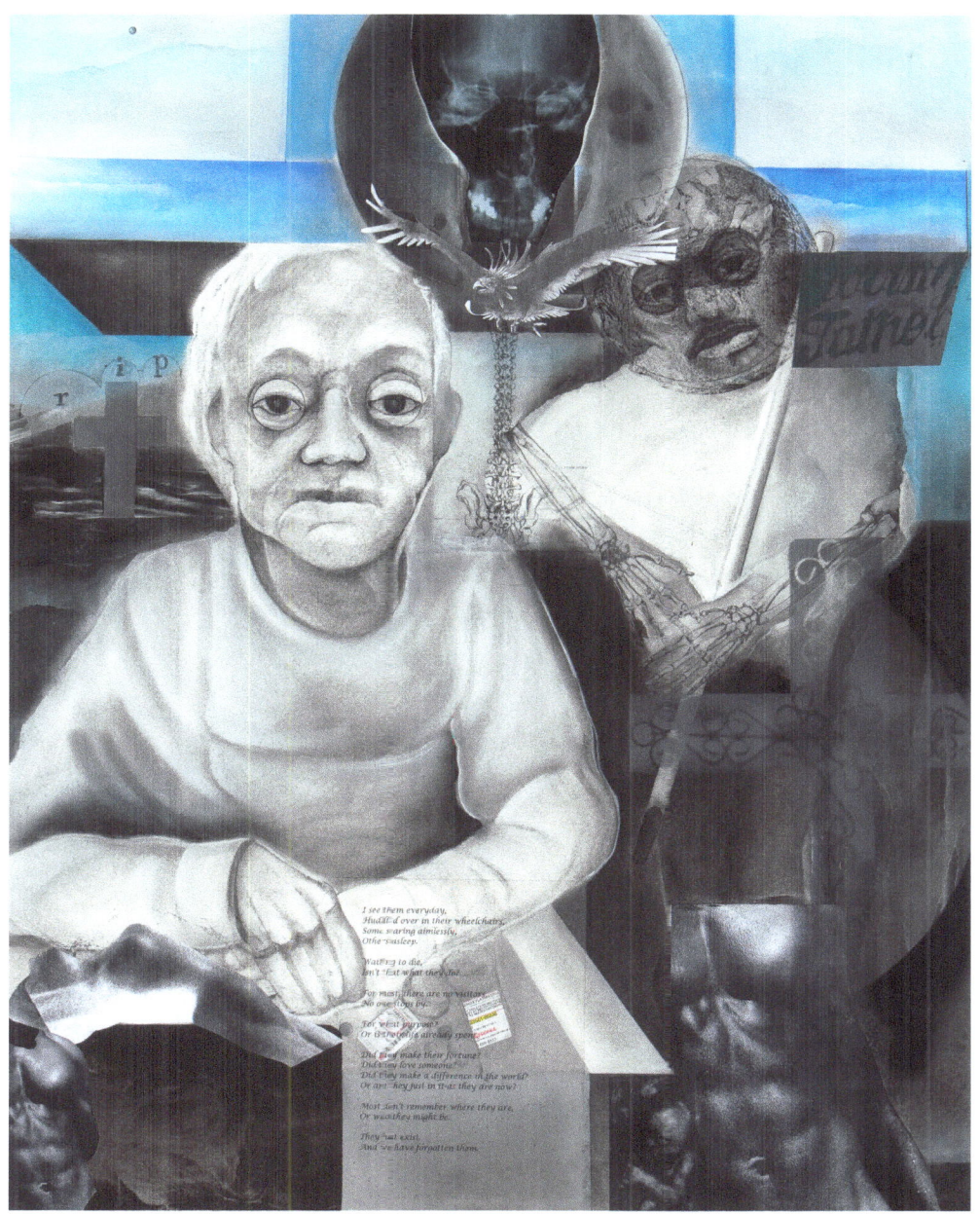

"Waiting to Die", Charcoal & Pastel

You Once Were Young

You once were young
    And vibrant...
Ninety-six years has
    Taken its toll,
There you lay,
A lovely soul.
Was your life
    Worthwhile?
Or did you just
    Exist?
Only God knows.
Sleep well my
    Friend.

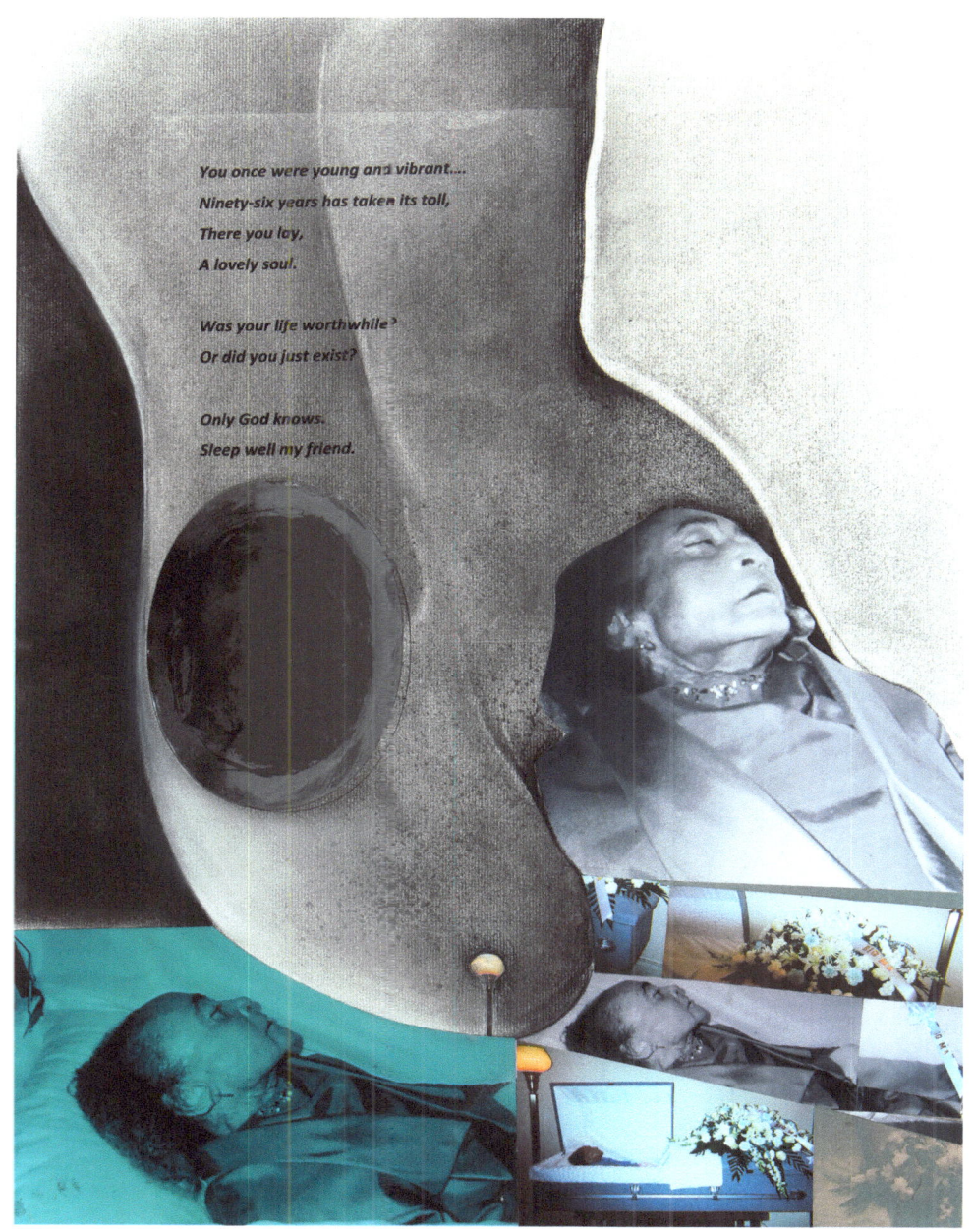

"You Once Were Young", Charcoal

About the Author

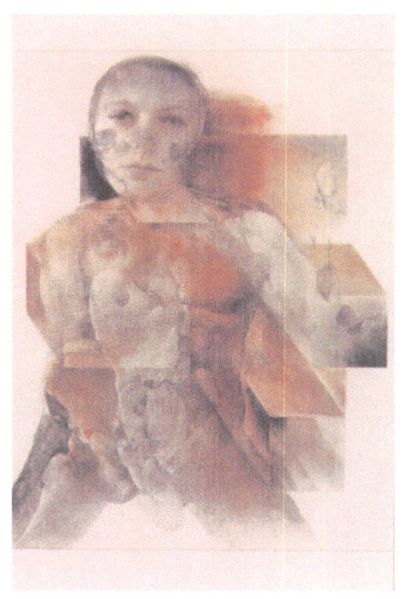

I was a caregiver for my husband who had vascular dementia for 15 years. Seven years ago he went into a nursing facility. I visited every day. I became acutely aware of the disease and its consequences. As an artist, I have executed seven drawings about Alzheimer's with seven accompanying poems that illustrate the seven stages of its progression. Since his death, it is my intention to share this information with those individuals whose loved ones have been recently diagnosed with the disease. For more information, visit www.alz.org/gmc

Pat Duff is a Detroit-based artist. To view more of her artwork, visit PatDuffArt.com

www.ingramcontent.com/pod-product-compliance
Lightning Source LLC
Chambersburg PA
CBHW051839210526
45473CB00005B/1940